What's the Buzz?

Honey for a Sweet New Year

This **PJ BOOK** belongs to

_____

_____

PJ Library®

JEWISH BEDTIME STORIES and SONGS

By Allison Ofanansky

Photos by Eliyahu Alpern

KAR-BEN
PUBLISHING

To my husband Shmuel and daughter Aravah, I love you both.
Wishing many sweet years to all the kids in this book.
— A.O.

To my loving family Nili, Yagel, and Nitzan and to Robert Hayutin z"l
— E.A.

Many thanks to the staff at the Dvorat Hatavor Bee Farm and Education Center for
their warm welcome and for allowing us to photograph there
Visit Dvorat Hatavor at www. dvorat-hatavor.co.il.

Text copyright © 2011 Allison Ofanansky
Photos copyright © 2011 by Eliyahu Alpern www.tziloom.com

Kar-Ben Publishing
A division of Lerner Publishing Group, Inc.
241 First Avenue North
Minneapolis, MN 55401 U.S.A.
1-800-4-KARBEN

Website address: www.karben.com

Library of Congress Cataloging-in-Publication Data

Ofanansky, Allison.
 What's the buzz? : honey for a sweet new year / by Allison Ofanansky ; photographed by Eliyahu Alpern.
    p. cm.
 Summary: A class in Israel tours a farm to learn about how honey is made and used to celebrate the Jewish New Year, Rosh
Hashanah.
 ISBN 978-0-7613-5640-0 (lib. bdg. : alk. paper) [1. Honeybee--Fiction. 2. Bees--Fiction. 3. Honey--Fiction. 4. School field
trips--Fiction. 5. Rosh ha-Shanah--Fiction. 6. Israel--Fiction.] I. Alpern, Eliyahu, ill. II. Title. III. Title: What is the buzz?
 PZ7.O31Wh 2011
 [E]--dc22
                                2010026181

Manufactured in China
1-43694-33487-2/7/2017

081720.2K1/B1074/A8

Our bus pulls up next to a sign with a big bee on it, and a man wearing baggy white coveralls comes aboard.

"Shalom. Welcome to our bee farm." He smiles. "I'm Yigal, and today we're going to learn how bees make honey."

My friends and I rush off the bus, but Amit hesitates. "I'm afraid of getting stung!" he calls after us.

"The bees won't hurt you," Yigal assures us, as we gather around him on picnic benches. "They're off in a room surrounded by glass. I wear this special suit to protect me when I go inside."

Yigal lights a fire in a little can. Smoke begins to puff out. "This will help keep the bees away from me."

Yigal puts on a funny hat with a screen over his face. Then he puts on long, thick gloves.

"He looks like an astronaut!" Stav giggles.

We follow Yigal down
the path to the hives.

He opens the lid of a hive and pulls out a flat tray. It is covered with hundreds and hundreds of bees!

We press our noses against the glass and watch.
Gaya says she sees the queen bee, but all the
bees look the same to me.

The bees go in and out of the honeycomb. Sticky honey drips from the compartments.

"How do bees make all those little compartments?" Noah asks. "With their feet or their wings?"

"Neither," Yigal explains. "They poke their heads into the soft wax to make little indentations."

"I've seen beehives like that in a field near my house," I say.

"Beekeepers put hives in lots of orchards and farms," Yigal explains. "That way the bees can sip nectar from different kinds of flowers and make different types of honey."

Yigal comes out of the glass room and takes off his hat.

"What's that?" Ido asks, pointing to a metal tub with a crank.

"People once used machines like these to get honey out of the honeycombs," Yigal explains. "As the tub spins around, the honey is sucked out of the little wax compartments."

He lets us each take a turn at the crank. It's fun, but I think it would get tiring after awhile.

"Now we use machines with engines," Yigal says. "But let's go inside and we'll talk about how the bees make honey."

We enter a small room decorated with pictures of bees, and take seats on low benches. Yigal holds out a plastic bee.

"Thousands of bees live in each hive," he says. "There are girl and boy bees and a queen. The girl bees do all the work. They sip the nectar from the flowers, bring it back to the hive, and make the honey. The girls also make wax to build honeycombs in the hive. And they care for the babies and the queen."

"What does the queen do?" Ari asks.

"The queen lays eggs. Lots and lots of eggs."

"What's left for the boy bees to do?" Amit asks.

"Not much," Yigal answers. "They sit around the hive eating honey and hoping to marry the queen." Sara giggles.

"Who wants to help?" he asks. We all raise our hands. Yigal gives me the little bee and hands flowers to Chaim and Noam.

I fly my bee from Chaim's flower to Noam's as Yigal begins to explain.

"Honey is made from nectar. Bees sip nectar from flowers using their long tongues. When their stomachs are full, they return to the hive and pass the nectar to other bees who turn it into honey.

"While they are sipping nectar, the bees also help the flowers," Yigal continues. "They pick up bits of pollen on their feet and transfer them to other flowers, so the plant can make fruit and seeds. I like to say the bees carry 'kisses' from flower to flower." We all laugh.

We learn that a bee can make ten or more trips a day back and forth to the hive. It is such hard work that she lives for only a month and makes just one teaspoon of honey in her lifetime.

"Wow," says Gaya. "It takes a lot of bees . . . "

" . . . and a lot of flowers," Rotem adds.

Yigal shows us the electric machine that
collects the honey. He turns a spigot
and fills little cups.

We all get a taste.

Then we move to long tables and Yigal hands out sheets of beeswax. They have a pattern on them like the pattern of the honeycomb. I carefully roll up my sheet of beeswax around a string wick to make a candle.

Rotem finishes her candle first.

Before we leave, we stop at the store. The shelves are filled
with jars of honey.

I pick out a jar of wildflower honey for my family. Then
I buy another jar for my friend Ruth who couldn't come
because she was sick.

The next day, I pick ripe apples from a tree in our garden. I put a few in a basket along with the jar of honey and bring them to Ruth's house.

While I tell her all about the day at the bee farm, we share apples dipped in honey. I wish Ruth a sweet new year and tell her I hope she feels better soon.

On the eve of Rosh Hashanah, I light my beeswax candle. My ima and abba and I all dip slices of apple in honey from the bee farm, and wish each other *shana tova u'metukah!* A happy and sweet year.

FUN FACTS

It is a tradition on Rosh Hashanah, the Jewish New Year, to eat apples or challah dipped in honey as a wish for a sweet new year.

Apples have been grown in Israel for over 4000 years. They are mentioned in *The Song of Songs* in the Bible. In Israel apples are grown primarily in the Galilee and Golan. Further south, it is too hot and dry for apples.

In the Torah, Israel is called "the land of milk and honey," because its climate is ideal for grazing animals and growing flowers.

People have collected honey from bees since prehistoric times. In Tel Rehov archeologists found clay beehives which are over 3000 years old!

In Israel today, there are more than 90,000 beehives in over 6,000 locations around the country. Most of the honey they produce is sold at Rosh Hashanah time.

To make one pound (half a kilogram) of honey, bees must collect nectar from two million flowers.

Honey is only one of the products bees make for us. They also produce royal jelly and propolis, used for cosmetic and medicinal purposes.

Bees are in danger! In the past few years, millions of bees all around the world have been dying from a variety of causes. If you want to help the bees, grow organic flowers in your yard!

ABOUT ROSH HASHANAH

Rosh Hashanah, the Jewish New Year, is celebrated in the autumn. Jewish people wish each other *"shanah tovah,"* a good new year. The challah eaten on Rosh Hashanah is different from the one eaten on Shabbat and other holidays. It is round, to remind us of the cycle of the year. Slices of challah and apples are dipped in honey to represent our wish for a sweet year. In the synagogue, prayers are recited from a special High Holiday prayerbook, and the shofar (ram's horn) is sounded during the service.

ABOUT THE AUTHOR

Allison Ofanansky, born in the U.S., moved to Israel and became an Israeli citizen in 1996. She lives in the village of Kaditah near the mystical city of Safed, with her husband Shmuel and daughter Aravah. They enjoy hiking the hills of the Galilee, gathering and eating the fruits that grow there. They are involved in environmental and eco-peace projects. This book is the third in her Jewish holiday series with photographer Eliyahu Alpern that includes *Harvest of Light* and *Sukkot Treasure Hunt*, both named Sydney Taylor Notable Children's Books.

ABOUT THE PHOTOGRAPHER

Born and raised outside Chicago, photographer Eliyahu Alpern has been interested in food, travel, and photography since childhood. He's been a musician, cougar rehabilitator, vegetarian chef, organic farmer, and multi-media maven. His photographic specialty is 360-degree panoramic images of Israel. He lives in the Upper Galilee with his wife, children, cat, and dog.